MY LIFE'S JOURNEY IS ONLY A TEST

Written and Edited by
TONYA Y. BEST

iUniverse, Inc.
New York   Bloomington

MY LIFE'S JOURNEY IS ONLY A TEST

iUniverse books may be ordered through booksellers or by contacting:

iUniverse
1663 Liberty Drive
Bloomington, IN 47403
www.iuniverse.com
1-800-Authors (1-800-288-4677)

Because of the dynamic nature of the Internet, any Web addresses or links contained in this book may have changed since publication and may no longer be valid.

ISBN: 9781450238922 (sc)
ISBN: 9781450238939 (ebk)

Printed in the United States of America

iUniverse rev. date: 6/18/2010

Contents

ACKNOWLEDGMENTS

To my daughters, SIERRA and DIAMONDS, I love you with every inch of my heart. This book is to encourage you that you can do anything that you set your mind to. Stay encouraged and never give up. I love you always.

To my friend, JONATHAN, I thank you for helping me on this book. At times when I wanted to give up you never let me. I thank you for the editing and support that you gave me. I truly don't know how I would have made it without your help.

To my cousin, SHABARBARA, I thank you for giving me the information that I needed to get this book out of my drawer and into publication. If it wasn't for your publishing your book, I don't know if I would have ever published mine. So I thank you from the bottom of my heart.

To my best friend, APRIL, thank you for believing in me and this book even when I didn't think it could happen. You always encouraged me to write. I thank you for being my support system, my backbone, my shoulder to cry on. You are truly my best friend, my sister. I love you with all my heart.

Most important, I thank GOD for being head of my life. May he rule and reign in my life forever. When everyone else could only see the worst in me, he looked through it all and saw the best in me. I thank God for being the biggest part of my life. Thank you for giving me another chance. I am so ever grateful.

Proud Moments

I was so proud the day you were born.
You were like my very own SUN,
So full of light that shines so bright.
As I watched you grow, only God knows
How much you mean to me.
On my knees I did bow.
I asked God to show you how,
To spread your wings so you could fly.
And, yes, on this day I will cry.
Baby, you are my joy forever,
My dream come true.
My happiness is you.
On this day I consider myself
The luckiest mom in the world
To have such a perfect little girl.
To make you smile does my heart proud.
I love you today and always.

My Girls

The first time I saw you I couldn't help but cry.
Right then you became the apples of my eye.
You had the prettiest brown eyes and the cutest button nose.
You were so little, so sweet that no one could compete.
I loved to watch you smile, I loved to watch you play.
You were the sunshine that brightened my day.
At night I would watch you sleep and that's when I would pray.
I would thank God for sending these little angels my way.
I showered you with love from the heavens up above.
I showed you that I loved you,
I showed you that I care,
I will show you that I will always be there.

TO MY DAUGHTERS WITH ALL MY LOVE.

On Your Birthday

As you turn twelve …
I have watched you crawl.
I listened to you say your first words.
I watched you take your first steps.
You have grown from a toddler, to a little girl, now to a preteen.
You are now at the age when things begin to happen with you—
After-school activities, trips to the mall, or just hanging with your friends.
You are now a little lady.
If I could turn back the hands of time
I would shield you from all the hurt and pain life throws your way.
I would give my life to make sure you are happy
Each and every day.

A Mother's Love

My girls are special to me.
The thought of them warms my heart.
They brighten my day
In every single way.
What more can I say?

They are:
MY LOVE
MY LIFE
MY WORLD
MY GIRLS

MY EVERYTHING…

My Daughters

Oh, Lord, please help me not to cry, for I must tell my two daughters why.

To my daughters, I love you to my last cry and life's final breath.

I love you till God calls me home and I have to say good-bye.

I know that you may be filled with hurt, pain, and tears, but remember that God has been with you through all of these years.

Although you may not understand, and you don't really know why, just bow your head and God will tell you why.

But never question God, and always believe, and through him you will always achieve all of your hopes and all of your dreams.

Like I have always said, God can handle anything,

So don't give up now and don't you ever cry.

I will always be the apple in your eye.

I will always be in your hearts.

I will always be in your dreams.

I feel our love can handle anything.

So stand up straight and keep your head held high.

With God you will always reach the sky.

Half Sisters

Half sisters we are, half sisters we may be,
But who would know just to see?
I have loved you from the start
Because God planted the seed in my heart
To make us sisters from the start.
Although I know you can't always be there,
You have always seemed to care
Even when no one else was there.
You have always had my back;
You even gave me just a little slack.
Even though you are a million miles away,
I just really want to say
That I love you each and every day.
Thank you for brightening up my day,

MY SISTER, MY COUSIN, MY FRIEND.

My Best Friend

I know I don't see you or talk to you every day
But I think of you whether you're near or far away.
I wonder how you're doing and what's going on.
I wonder if anyone's bothering you and if you're holding on.
I thank you for being my friend.
I thank you for being my girl.
I thank you for being a part of my world.
You have been there for me from the beginning to the end.
We've shared a lot of laughter.
We've shed a lot of tears.
We've overcome a lot of obstacles,
Overcome a lot of fears.
I thank God for you, for being there for me throughout the years,

MY BEST FRIEND.

Don't You Know?

Don't you know that I love you?
Don't you know that I care?
Don't you know that I will always be there
Through thick and thin, through ups and downs?
Don't you know that I will always be around,
To have your back and to take up all of your slack?
I bet you didn't know that you had it like that.
Through life's triumphs, if you should ever fall,
I will be there to help you stand tall.
So on my knees I did fall.
GOD said he would be there whenever I called.

Friends

Friends may come, friends may go—this is one thing that I do know.

But there is one friend who is always around when it seems no one else can be found.

You may feel as though your back is against the wall.

You may feel as though you're going to fall.

God is there to carry you through.

He always knows just what to do.

He has the power to pick you up and turn you around.

He can plant your feet on solid ground.

Forever

Forever I will love you.

Forever I will care.

Forever I will always be there.

Forever I will be yours.

Forever you will be mine.

Forever I will be yours till the end of time.

Fairy Tales Do Come True

How do you know when love is real?
How do you know love is true?
How do you know? Oh you just do.
I've always heard of love at first sight.
I never thought it could happen to me
Until this man walked up to me.
He asked me my name and where I lived.
I tried not to think of it as a really big deal.
As we started to talk he began to steal my heart.
I began to fall head over heels.
This new man of mine was a really big deal.
He makes me smile from deep within my soul
Till the point where I think it glows.
He makes me feel complete.
He makes me feel whole.
This new man of mine, I never want to let him go,
So whoever said fairy tales don't come true,
My fairy tale came true the moment I met you.

Lost Love

I had a good man but I just couldn't see
What God had placed right in front of me.
I regret the fact that I ever let him go
Because I didn't know
How much love he had for me since I couldn't see.
I let the man who I loved get away.
I was fed up and didn't know the right words to say
That would express the way that I feel,
To show him that my love was for real.
I just wanted him to propose to me
So that our love would always be.
I only wanted to be his wife
So that I could spend the rest of my life
With the man who I loved sent from the heavens up above.
I loved him in more ways than he could ever know.
Now there is no way that I can ever show him how I feel,
Because my feelings were for real.
Will this love that I still have for him ever end?
He wasn't only my lover, he was my very best friend.

I Feel

I feel as though I hurt you.

Tell me if that's true.

I feel as though I hurt you.

I can tell when I look at you.

I feel as though I hurt you.

I can see it in your eyes.

I feel as though I hurt you.

I heard you when you cried.

All I Want

I want to always be honest.

I want to always be true.

I never want to hurt you or make you feel blue.

I'll give you my heart.

I'll give you my soul,

For I want only you to hold.

Please hold me tight for the rest of my life,

Even when things don't seem to be going just right.

My Heart

The thought of you warms my heart.
Whether we're near or far apart
I think of you every day.
You're the sunshine that brightens my day.
I wonder sometimes if you feel me in your heart,
Because I don't ever want us to be apart.
You are a part of my heart.
You are a part of my soul.
You are what makes me whole.
I wonder if you'll always stay and never leave my side,
Because I want you here with me till the end of time.

A Prayer

Don't you know that I love you?

Don't you know that I care?

Don't you know that I whisper your name often in a prayer?

I said a prayer for you today because you were on my mind.

I said a prayer for you today. I hope it will ease your mind.

I said a prayer for you today that can stand the test of time,

For God said he would be there every single time.

My Lover, My Friend

I miss you when we're not together.

I want this feeling to last forever.

Please hold me tight if only for one night.

I want to be wrapped up in your arms, where I feel protected from all harm.

Please tell me how you feel and if the feelings are for real.

I miss you when we're apart because you have stolen my heart.

I never want this night to end for you aren't just my lover,

You're my very best friend.

A Friend of Mine

You said you could spoil me.
This much you have proven to be true.
You said you cared for me,
And I hope and pray that you do.
You told me to never look back because you would never leave my side.
You were even there to hold me at times when I cried.
Do you want me to say that I love you?
Do you want me to say that I care?
Do you want me to say thank you for always being there?
I will say that I love you.
I will say that I care.
I will say thank you for always being there.

Tell Me

You call me your friend and not your girl.
Tell me if I'm the center of your world.
How long should this friendship last?
Tell me if it will ever change.
Tell me if I will ever have your last name.
Tell me if I will ever be yours.
Tell me if you will ever be mine
Tell me if this love can stand the test of time.
Tell me if you want me to go.
Tell me if you want me to stay.
Tell me if you want me to pack my bags and simply walk away.
Tell me how you feel and if the feeling is real.
Tell me your life's history so we can bond,
And I'll tell you mine so we can belong.
Tell me now because this is a really big deal.
Tell me now if this love is for real.
Do you love me? The thing is I don't really think you do.
Tell me the truth whether or not it makes me sad and blue.
I know that I'm not your lover,
But tell me there is no other.

Wasted Time

I need to stop wasting so much time on you
When there is so much more that I can do.
I wait for your arrival,
I wait for you call,
Only for you to not show up at all.
It seems like you always have so much to do,
Places to go and people to see,
That you forget all about me.
You are the biggest part of my life,
So why does it seem like I'm the least important part of yours?
Maybe I just want too much.
When all I really want is
To be yours.

If

When you look at me tell me what you see.

Do you understand my story?

If I told you that I loved you, would you even care?

If I told you that I needed you, would you be there?

If I told you my hopes and dreams, would you ask me, what's that suppose to mean?

Sometimes when I talk I may begin to fuss.

I know that you only want me to hush.

When I talk, do you even listen?

Or do you wish I would just disappear?

Sometimes you act as though I'm not even here.

You Tried to Hold Me Down

You tried to hold me down.
You told me I would never succeed.
Who are you to judge me and what I can achieve?
You told everyone I was no good.
You said this without a doubt.
You even scandalized my name
Like you knew what I was all about.
Who are you to judge me or to even call me out of my name?
Who are you to even use my name in vain?
All my life I've had to struggle.
All my life I've had to fight.
Who knew my life would be like this without a shadow of a doubt?
I have always tried my best to do as I should.
I have always tried to just be good.
I'm just waiting to hear Jesus say,
"Well done, my good and faithful servant,
Welcome home. You've done good."

Dilemma

What one won't do.

Another one will.

When one feels as though their back is against the wall,

The other is trying to give their all.

One is feeling pressure and doesn't want to change,

While the other wants to give you their last name.

I guess you will have to make a choice.

I guess you will have to decide

At which residence you will reside.

Just a Man

I was in a relationship with this guy—
I can't even begin to tell you why.
He started out making me feel like his love was for real,
But actually to him it was no big deal.
He wasn't meant for me and this much I tried not to see,
Because he became a part of me.
I should have known it would never last,
Because of the things that happened in the past.
He hurt me in the worst way
To the point that I had nothing to say.
He doesn't realize it still hurts till this day.
He had an affair right in my face.
You could see the pain all over my face.
I questioned him and asked him why.
He looked at me as if to say "Why?"
Or "How dare you ask me about anything that I've done!"
As if he had done nothing wrong.
I was a fool and took him back,
Only for him to stab me once again in my back.

Single

I was told the reason why I wasn't married, was because I was too picky.

This only made me realize, this only made me see,

That the relationship that I wanted will never be.

Maybe that's the reason why he always called me his baby and not his girl,

Always said that he cared for me, and that I was his girl,

Never that I was his world.

I Want

I want a man who
I can run to that will hold me tight,
Wipe my tears and tell me that everything will be all right.
I want a man who
Is proud to have me on his arm,
Where I feel protected from all harm.
I want a man who
Isn't afraid to tell his friends that I'm his girl, and not just a friend.
I want a man who
Is proud to say that I'm the center of his world.
I want a man who
Will hold my hand when we walk.
I want a man who
Will tell me that he loves me when we talk.

When

When a man says he loves you
Do you just want to walk away?
When a man says he loves you
Do you just want to kneel down and pray?
When a man says he loves you
Do you just want to break down and cry?
When a man says he loves you
Do you just want to sigh?
When a man says he loves you
Do you feel as though he said it in vain?
When a man says he loves you
Do you still feel all the pain?
When a man says he loves you
Do you feel as though you just can't take it anymore?
When a man says he loves you
Don't you just want to walk out of the door?

Invisible

I'm invisible. Why can't you see
That you can look straight through me?
My inner feelings are just a start of my broken heart.
My life is a mess but I think it's only a test
Of life's winding time, or is it just a rhyme?
Maybe it's just the end of time.
I can't eat, I can't sleep. What other dilemma will I meet?
I cry all the time. It feels like I'm losing my mind.
I have so many problems, I have so many fears.
My heart is filled with so many tears.
I've been down for oh so long.
I don't know how much longer I can hold on.
Sometimes I just want to die.
I'm not going to lie.
Sometimes I just want to break down and cry,
And I don't even know why.

Strength

I look and appear to be strong,

Although at times I'm weak.

Sometimes when I need to talk

I just can't seem to speak.

At night I cry when no one can see

Because that's the only time when I can truly be me.

I shed my tears to try and relieve the stress, to relieve the pain.

My flesh is weak, but my mind is strong.

I just need the strength to keep holding on.

A Cry for Help

I get so depressed.

I need a way out of this mess.

My life seems so low.

I don't know how much further I can go.

Sometimes my load gets so heavy

Till I don't know what to do.

I put my life in your hands,

For you're the only one who understands.

Only you can lead me to the promised land.

Alone

Sometimes I don't want to be bothered.

Sometimes I just want to be free.

Sometimes I just want some free time, some free time just for me.

Sometimes I just want to sit home, and not pick up the phone.

C'mon now! I said I just want to be left alone,

So stop bothering me, and get off my back.

Just leave me alone, and get up out of my face.

I said I just need some time and space.

So Alone

My heart is broken.

My heart is filled with tears.

I've been down for so many years.

Tell me what has went on

That my things have been taken.

Why is it that I get such dirty looks?

People talk behind my back.

I have to hear all that smack.

Tell me, how can I go on?

My Silence

When I don't talk, my silence should speak,

The gratitude of how I feel.

And, yes, my feelings are for real.

When I needed you the most you were not there.

You showed me right then that you didn't care.

I guess that's just a message to me, to just be aware

That this relationship isn't going anywhere.

I know that you say that you care, and that may be true.

Your actions most definitely say that you're not in love with me.

Hear My Cry

Lord, please take my pain away,
For I pray each and every day
That you help me find a way.
I know I don't always do as I should.
You have always understood.
You never let me go, you always held my hand.
I know what it feels like to want to die,
Although I know it won't solve anything, so I just sit and cry.
It helps to take some of the pain away.
Tears are God's way of cleaning the soul
Till the point where no one has to know.

Why Me?

Why is it that bad things happen to good people?
Why is it that everything I do seems like a slap in my face?
Why is it that my life seems so out of place?
I appear to be happy on the outside while my heart is breaking on the
inside.
I always feel like no one loves me and no one cares.
Why is it that I feel like no one is ever there,
When I know that God is always there?
He walks with me, he talks with me,
He tells me that everything will be okay.
He is there with me every single day.
When I go to bed at night
He tells me not to worry, that everything will be all right.

Judge

You can't judge me

When you don't even know me.

You only know what you heard.

You only know what you think you see.

You don't know the real me.

You don't know what I've been through.

You don't know what I'm made of.

You don't know my feelings.

You don't know my thoughts.

You don't know what's going on inside my heart.

Private

I have something to tell you.
I don't know where to start.
I have something to tell you.
I know it will break your heart.
I promised to always be honest.
I promised to always be true.
I promised to always tell you my feelings, my feelings for you.
But how do you tell someone you love that you won't always be around?
How do you tell them that you have to live apart,
That you have known from the very start?
If you walk away I'll understand.
After all, you are a grown man
Who deserves to be happy,
Who deserves to be sure
That he has a girl who is pure.

Stolen Innocence

I've always tried to be a good daughter.
I've always tried to be a good girl.
Tell me what happens when someone comes in and breaks down your world,
When someone takes your innocence away.
Tell me why no one is there to tell you that everything will be okay.
Who will be there to help you with all the hurt?
Who will be there to help you with all the pain?
Who will be there to help you not to go insane?
Who will be there to wipe the tears away?
Who will be there to say there will be a brighter day?

Why?

Why didn't you help me?
Why didn't you protect me?
Why didn't you hear me crying?
Why didn't you see me dying?
Why didn't you see my pain?
Why didn't you see me going insane?
Why didn't you see my tears?
After all of these years
I still needed your help.
I even called out your name.
I needed your help
To handle all of this pain.

The Secrets that We Share

How does it feel to try to be me?
How does it feel to try to take my place?
How does it feel to step inside my world?
You thought you could be me.
You thought you could be his girl.
How does it feel to know that you weren't the center of his world?
You thought if you told lies and talked down about me, it would win his heart,
When it was only the start to your broken heart.
It all blew up in your face, when he said that you all could only be friends.
I bet you felt like a fool for what you had just did.
He told me all about it, even what you had said and done.
Remember, he wasn't just my lover; he was my very best friend.
That kind of bond you can't break down
No matter what you may do or say.
We still talk and are friends till this day.

Anything Is Possible

God saved my soul.
He made me whole.
He forgave me for all of my sins
So I can live again
From the beginning to the end.
He was my friend.
He never judged me.
He even gave me a second chance
So now I can dance.
I will praise him in advance
For giving me a second chance.

God Is Using Me

God is always busy. God is always opening doors.
I have to be thankful that he loves me even more.
I know this without a doubt.
My God will surely bring me out.
I don't want your pity.
I don't want your sympathy.
I know my God is looking after me.
God saw the best in me.
He looked beyond all my flaws.
I thank you, God, for giving me your all.

Power

I'll never know your true powers.

I'll never know your true plans.

I do know that you hold my life in the palm of your hand.

I don't always do what's right.

I know I do a lot that's wrong.

But as long as I walk with you

I can lean on your everlasting arm.

I don't always know what to do or where to go.

All I can do is try to stay on the straight and narrow

So I can follow you wherever you go.

You Were There

You were there when I was up.

You were there when I was down.

You were there when no one else was around.

You told me to keep my head up.

You told me to never look down.

You told me that God is always around.

You told me to pray and to believe.

You told me that I must have faith the size of a mustard seed.

You told me to never give up and to always keep the faith

Because that's what I will need to run this race.

People

People think they know my life.

People think they know my story.

I really have to thank God for all his glory.

He brought me from a mighty long way.

This much I have to say.

When I look back over my life

I see where I came from.

I have to thank God for all he has done.

I have truly been blessed.

I HAVE TRULY BEEN BLESSED.

Oh, Lord, Hear My Cry

Oh, Lord, please hear my cry, for I don't know why

I experience so much hurt, why I experience so much pain.

I do know that you are an amazing God that can handle anything.

I know that I shouldn't worry, and that I shouldn't fret.

You are an amazing God that has never failed me yet.

I know that you will protect me from all hurt and harm.

That's why I'm leaning on your everlasting arm.

I know that you are a God of second chances.

That's why I'm putting my life in your hands.

With you I know I will make it to the promise land.

Pray

It's time to pray, or didn't you know?
I guess you forgot, so I'll have to show
You how to pray in the middle of the night,
When things don't seem to be going just right.
I heard you call out just the other day.
Oh Lord, please show me how to pray.
On my knees I did pray for God to send an angel her way,
To shower her with love from the heavens up above.
Give her mercy and grace to carry her through.
Lord, I know you'll know just what to do.
Please bless her heart, so she'll know where to start.
Give her strength to pray each and every day.
Let her remember this day oh Lord I pray.

What Can I Say?

I don't know the right words to say that may brighten your day.

All I can do is pray that God sends an angel your way

To shower you with love from the heavens up above.

Although your heart may be hurting and your eyes filled with tears,

Remember God is with you—he has been for years.

He has never left your side. He has even wiped your weeping eyes.

He knows your hurts. He knows your pains.

With God you can make it through anything.

Weak

Your spirit is strong

But your body is weak.

Sit on down and rest your feet.

Give God time to work.

Give God time to heel.

You do know God is real.

Fly Away

If I could fly away

Up to heaven I would go.

I would marvel in all its glory.

It would be such a beautiful story.

Up in heaven is where I want to stay,

Where I could live each and every day.

Don't be mad because I want to fly away.

I pray that you can come and join me in heaven some sweet day.

I Thank You

Lord, I thank you
For waking me up this morning,
For starting me on my way.
Lord, I thank you for just another day.
Lord, I thank you
For the sun and the moon,
For the stars in the sky.
Lord, I thank you for being the star in my eye,
For guiding me on my way. Thank you for brightening up my day.
Lord, I thank you
For my life, health, and strength,
For my will to live, for the ability of my limbs.
Lord, I thank you
For blessing me with two beautiful girls,
For they are the center of my world.
For without you I don't know what I would do or where I would be.
I would be lost.
So many take life for granted. They don't realize your power
When you are there for us every single hour.

This book is to show you that I am just like you. We all have problems, but that only makes us stronger. This book conspired from some of the things that I went through in my life: raising two girls, experiencing backstabbing friends, and enduring disappointing relationships. The bible says that God won't put more on you than what he knows you can bear. So for that I say: God, I thank you for all I went through in my life. It has truly made me a stronger person. If it had not been for all the trials and tribulations I went through in my life, this book never would have happened.

This book consists of fifty-one poems on different things that happened over the period of my life. It is just to show you that life is a journey. We don't always have a say about the things that happen to us. We just have to live the hand that we were dealt. Where I came from you have to have the faith that any and everything is possible, and that there will be a brighter day. BE BLESSED.